TILL FOREVER FALLS APART

RAEMAN AIDASANI

mi cielito

saturn: my definition of life, *you.*

your love is the sweetest story written on the pages of my heart

you're my eternal muse

Contents

Contents

Contents

Contents

Contents

Preface

I'm just a girl who was born into an imperfect world. Life gives us all challenges shaping and molding us into who we are as humans. I was told my whole life that these challenges are Gods will, but the truth I learned is that Newtons law holds true, we all have free will, but for every action, there is an equal and opposite reaction, we go through life influencing and being influenced by others. These expereinces leave an impression sometimes small but also sometimes those impressions are everlasting. This is the story of how I learned to grow from my experince of love.

Acknowledgements

With deepest gratitude, I acknowledge my beloved parents. You'll always be the closest to my heart.

To my sister, I'll always be your first child.

To my best friends, who heard it first and pushed me to continue the story.

You are made of magic.

Aaditi Manwani

Esha Naidu

Jiya Somai

Tamanna Verma;

my stars, couldn't have done it without you all!

Prologue

love has many names
but you are by far my favorite

1. come over

come over

and ring the bell once and wait for what seems like an eternity

before I open the door

slowly lean onto me and dont worry about being too heavy

wrap your arms around me, sigh as loud as you can and refuse

to move an inch from where we stand

bury your nose in the nape of my neck and tell me that you

have missed me, that you missed this

I have made you soup, one that's so hot, it's going to burn

your insides so I shall carefully blow on

every spoon before I feed it to you

tell me that you give up and nothing in the world makes sense

anymore

gently wipe your mouth on the back of your palm and

surrender yourself in my lap and stay there as

long as you need, until the sun dips into the ocean and the

crickets chirp unanimously welcoming

the darkness

but don't go yet, it's my turn to breakdown

it's my turn to hit your chest and ask you what took you so

long to understand I am all that you need

and the world need not make sense because

tonight you're here with me under the fluffliest of white
blankets we've held each other the entire
time refusing to let go
and thats all I care for

2. you

you're the thought that starts each morning
the conclusion to each day
you are in all that I do
and everything I say
you're the smile on my face
the twinkle in my eye
the warmth inside my heart
the fullness in my life
you're the hand that's laced in mine
and the coat upon my back
my friend, my love
my shoulder to lean on
you're my silly, mature, caring,
thoughtful, bright, and honest guy
the one who holds me tightly
when I need to cry
you're the dimple in my cheek
the ever-constant tingle in my soul
the voice that makes me weak
the happiness of my life
you are all I've wanted
you are all I need
you are all I've dreamed of

3. my love

my love
don't you see
how the snow falls gently
resolving into water at the slightest touch of nature
what makes you believe, you are not enough?
when you are a part of nature's greatest magic
rising like your mother
in seasons

4. lover

I never thought I'll be a lover
but
I could make a religion
out of how I imagined us doing the dishes together

5. celestial ties

my love,

what else can I offer that I have not already given?

how many poems can I write?

how many words can I speak?

how many times can I hold and be held

run my hands across your cheeks

sing to the stars of your eyes?

tell me what you want and I will seek it out

for none of this feels enough

for someone who means so much

no earthly thing exists to give and gift

to adequately express such a internal thrum

a swelling storm

a night blooming garden forever stretching towards your light

there is a part of me that aches

beautifully, longingly, intensely

they say-

this is what it means to truly love

6. damon salvatore

and when I go out with you for the first time

I hope the pink in the sky matches the red in my cheeks

I hope there's too many words for us to say over one cup of coffee

I hope time runs out like an upside-down sand clock so

we must make up for the words unsaid by sitting awfully close to each other

in complete silence and hoping our hearts can calm down at some point

I hope the sound of your laugh wraps all around me and keeps me warm

if not, you could always offer your jacket and be the gentleman

that the world claims you are

I hope whilst we talk more about life and damon salvatore

I get to find it in my heart to say that you're all that I think about sometime's

always actually, I correct myself, I think about you constantly

I hope we forget about our coffee and focus on far more important things

such as hands that have to be urgently held and

hair that needs to be caressed back behind the ear

I hope you know I am always dying inside when you're looking at me
that it makes my day when you come say hi
I hope you read my poems someday and i hope you gently find yourself in them
and lastly I hope I get to say all of this to you when I see you

7. horizon

I am your moon
you are my sea
somehow entwined
somehow far apart
a half dozen planets
a half dozen worlds or so
could fit between us skin to skin
but there goes the tide
in rise and fall
like breathing in living lungs
and there goes our gravity undeniable
like heartbeats and long lifelines
to love, to love, to love
until we meet at the horizon
magnetism of salted skin
reflected light
our limbs entwined
at last
the world will wait for us

8. soul ties

I want to talk to you
and hear about your day
I want to listen to your heart
while on your chest I lay
I want to interlock hands
kiss your lips
and whisper into your ear
to tell you that I've got you, always
I want you to know that
I wont leave you during
this lifetime or the next
because I intend for our souls to never part ways

9. all too well

I secretly imagined a future with you
we'd slow dance around an empty room
at four in the morning with a smile clinging to our faces
life would never grow to be boring as long as I was with you
you'd make me laugh on days I couldnt remember to smile
I'd fall asleep in your arms everyday and night
because they'd remind me of how it feels to be safe
and there is no one that can replace you
you have the most wonderful heart I've ever known
you're worth everything to me and more

10. yours

you're the music that keeps me dancing
the humor in a joke that keeps me laughing
you're the movie I want no ending to
my favorite book that I'll keep on reading
your smile is intoxicating
maybe even liberating
this is no exultation
I was made to be yours

11. pg.113

through poetry
I released up bottled up feelings
I get to scream I miss you
without embarrassment
all the ugly and the sad
are less mortifying
I get to tell you
I love you
without cowardice
I lose and find myself
in between lines of confession and metaphors
that all lead to you
and we meet at page
hundred and thirteen to talk about your day
like I haven't already got a clue

12. muse

I've never met someone so impressive in so many more ways
than one
and one day they will write historical articles about everything
you've done
lights dim in cmparison
hurricanes fear such a force
and maybe you never wanted to be a muse but
you're my inspirational source

13. heart to heart

I've met with your shadows and I don't mind them
we all learn to dance with devils somewhere along the way to
heaven
you're not a fallen angel but everything about you feels holy
even the parts you cast away, I'll take it
I'll kiss your insecurities till you're naked
your love could never hurt me
not when you are the one I prayed for
someone must've listened
maybe I'll meet them one day
I see as the trees wink at me, the universe knows something
they know I need your light
from sun to midnight
as we grow towards each other like flowers finding their hands
dont fall over, I'll help you stand
hush, I'm right here, simply ask
our love can be slow, but my heart
my heart is fast

14. phases

you are my moon
- *I love you in all your phases*

15. close

my mother always told me
that when you find the one person in this world
whose weirdness matches your own
keep them close
how do I politely tell you
that you are the most
strangely, unique
human being
that I have ever met
and it is every reason why
you are the only thing living
inside my head?

16. roses

you paint my roses red
when I thought I'd have to spend a lifetime
just being blue
-I didn't know someone could make me feel the way that you
do

17. senselesss

when nothing
in this world
makes sense
his existence does
sometimes
his presence
in my world
is the only thing that makes sense

18. every part of me

you are every part of me
I dont know if that makes sense to you,
but it makes sense to me
because every part of you
is the home I never knew I would need
because the only words I can write
are about what your love does for me
because all of you
has become
every part of me
and from what I can see
even the most perfectly curated
strings of words
could never depict
that you are the only thing
I could ever need
because you are
the only part of me
that I was ever missing
- and I dont know if that makes sense to you,
but you make sense to me

19. eternal melody

under the moon's gentle glow, my heart flows
a silent river of love, only the night knows
in your laughter, my every dream begins to spin
a dance of joy, where true love takes us in
like Ghalib's verses, deep and profound
in your eyes, a universe I found
our love, a secret the stars silently keep
a connection so deep, it speaks when words sleep
your presence, a warmth in life's embrace
in the canvas of love, together we trace
a poetic verse of love, forever bold
in you, my song, my poem, so right
with you my heart finds it's light
in love's language we find our verse
in this vast universe, our love, so diverse

20. inseparable

have I told you I hate texting?
let me come caress your face and put you to sleep
while hearing your little snores
let me cook for you
and feed you spoons full of love
let me melt in your arms
till we're one
inseparable
cosmic creation

21. safe

she felt so safe opening up to him
as if she was opening up to herself
confronting her deeper thoughts she had always tried to hide
from
"I want connection," she began to say, "it's what I want the
most but I disconnect so easily,"
she paused for a second, not sure if she wanted to reveal any
more
because it would be so much easier to her thoughts hidden
but she continued,
"and I think it's because...I don't feel I am worthy of
connection and of...being loved"
and without hesistation, he told her
"but you are worthy"
he said it as if it were a fact
"you've changed my life...
and that is worth something"

22. worthy

I will love you through everything and anything
I will love you when you feel your best
and feel worthy of love and of being seen
I will love you when you go through huge milestones
and accomplisments and are living your dreams
I will love you when you feel your worst and feel unworthy of
love
and want to push everyone away
I will show you how worthy you are of love that will stay
I will love you in the everyday moments
while you are simply existing
you are enough as you are in every single way
and I will show you how you are worthy of love,
not only when you feel your best, but every second and
everyday
without ever depending on what you accomplish and do
but solely because you are you
this is how I will always love you and
you deserve to love youself in this way too

23. ever-changing

things are always changing
and I know my life willl change in the years to come
but I know one thing that will always remain constant
and that is your presence in my life
I know you will always be there for me and I for you
a lot of things break or being to fade away over time
but I know our connection will only grow stronger
and I promise you my love for you will never fade
because my love for you will continue to grow
every
single
day

24. oh to be loved

oh to be loved like a habit and not a chore
oh to be loved because loving you is their default state of being
and not something they have to perform like a duty
oh to be loved because they don't want to live a life
where loving you doesn't exist
oh to be loved truly

25. finally

it was windy the day we met...
turns out it was the universe breathing a sigh of relief
as she whispered,
"finally"

26. soft smile

you asked me today
how much I love you
and I sat for a moment
trying to conjure the right words
until eventually
I told you
that if I could start my life over
the only thing I would change
is perhaps a soft smile
kept on my face
as I venture down my path of trauma
knowing your hand
waits outstretched for me in the end

27. sometimes

sometimes
loving you is as simple as
watching the moon
sometimes
it's as difficult as counting the stars
but I love doing both for you

28. eyes

my eyes cannot see a thing
without noticing some part of you
and my heart cannot beat a second
without feeling some trace of you
and my mind cannot move an inch
without bumping into some memory of you

29. looks

the way he looks at me
makes me feel like the moon
shining just because the sun looks at you
I want to make perfume
out of the way he looks at me
so I can carry it with me all day and
only have to breathe in whenever I feel ugly
I want to cover myself uo
with the way he looks at me
so that I'm never cold again
and I were to bury
the way he looks at me on a field
it would be full of dandelions next spring

30. tell me

tell me
about all the places
on your body
that you keep avoiding
so I can visit them
admire them
and make them your favourite

31. need

I don't dance much
but with you
I have just enough courage
in the kitchen
when the right song comes on
and nobody else is around
I don't cook much
but with you
I'll peel every potato
shred every block of cheese
and wash every dish
when we're through
I don't sleep much
but I think I could
fall asleep next to you
into deep dreams
where I can be again
with you
I don't need much
but I really need you

32. I cannot

the only way my heart knows to go
is down
my love cannot swim
only dive and drown
I cannot kiss you
without losing my breath
I cannot look at you
without drowning in your eyes
I cannot kiss you
without choking on my desire
and I cannot love you
without forgetting myself

33. you scare away the darkness

you scare away the darkness
in the morning
when the sun peeks out from behind the curtain
and finds my face
that's how it feels when you look at me
like I'm sleeping and you tickle my nose
and I squeeze my eyes
because I'm not used to life being this bright
you scare away the darkness
put a spot of light on me
and I feel like an animal after hibernation
finished, thirsty, hungry for life

34. lifetime

I'd still recognize you in total darkness
were you mute and I blind
I'd still find you in another lifetime
like the tides seek the moon
but if there's a universe where you don't exist
I'd have to live a life essentially purposeless
you eclipse me, and in your shadows, I fumble for my
own significance
your absence hollows me out, leaving me a shell
questioning it's own resonance
without you I'm a wandering echo
yearing for the harmony of our interlinked existence

35. talker

I was always the talker, but I could always stare into your
cinnamon tinted eyes
and dream, stealing a glance here and there if it means to get
a peak of your smile crowned by your dimples
eyes are the windows of the soul they say,
would you see how much i'm willing to do for you
if we stare at each other for minutes?
or would it take hours
it's okay, we have all the time in the world
now I know, I would find you anywhere just by the small
speck
of gold in the upper corner of your orbs,
like honey pooling down
how am I a poet, if I can't write you a poem about
how they shine when you talk about the things you love
even if there isn't my name on that list
look at me
I beg
find the desperation holding my feelings hostage in my eyes,
the devotion playing tricks on my pupils and the admiration
creating
the glint on my irises
because eyes are the window to one's soul after all

36. how I love

this is how I love
I'd carry the sun on my back like the flesh off my back
than have it singe yours
this is how I love
I'd tie a lasso around the moon if you asked me to
show you the world
limitations matter little to me
this is how I love
Id find you five dimensions more before
I'd let you think
that you deserve any less than the very universe
we hurl through

37. prayer

I wrote your name in my handwriting
addressing your name felt like I've known you
the letter was half written
I won't sign in the end because
I wanna keep us going, like an endless letter
how chaotic the day was when I met you but
in the cold night hearing your voice felt warm
I love the feeling of knowing you
time was ticking buI I saw you waiting for me as I tie my
shoelaces
I felt like crying but i smiled through swollen eyes
you didn't see me but you saw parts of me
I didn't even show you
I was fine before you came
I'm happy since you've entered the spectrum of my heart, so
I knew I was falling but I wasn't scared
the walls of my room have heard me laugh the most
when I speak to you,
never knew I'd feel safe in my own bed
cause you were on the other side of the line
if I want to call you again I won't ask you
but I'll write a poem about you
somewhere you feel so loved

putting you in words might be my favourite thing and

I want to keep you in my life as you make me feel alive

is it just a name or prayer

38. unspoken

the tender touch of your hand on my waist
is an unspoken delight
it feels like falling from great heights, yet with you,
it's just right
goosebumps arise within, a silent shout of our secret
connection
every step we take down the lane, a thrilling direction
perhaps you're drawing my closer, or guiding me away
your hand lifts, then returns, in a sweet, subtle play
it's a gentle torment when your touch leaves it's rightful place
like forgetting my favourite song, lost in your embrace
the ache of not having you close, a longing that's profound
when you're near but not holding me, it's a love unbound
but from the moment we met, you claimed my heart's desire
so in the end, your love makes me the true victor, lifting me
higher

39. stardust

everything is stardust

you and I are made of what once burned hotter than anything
else in the universe

what gives light in the day and twinkled at night

but if I could pluck each star from its pedestal and make it
into a crown for you

it still wouldn't be the most radiant thing made of stardust in
the universe

because,

that's already you

40. don't you?

you love him, don't you?
what?
I don't know
I mean I guess
maybe
probably
but define love
describe love
is it the way my heart beats to the syllables of his name at the
thought of his existence
or the way the butterflies created a home in the pit of my
stomach because his energy
still makes me nervous
or is the way I once tried to dissolve this feeling I have for him
only to come back
twelve times stronger
then yes
I love him
I'm more than in love with him

41. you are not the world

you are sunlight falling through trees
you are laughter that breaks through sadness
you are the breeze on a too-warm day
you are clarity in the midst of confusion
you are not the world
but you are everything that makes the world good
without you, my life would still exist
but that's all it would manage to do

42. naked

for you, I am fragile
for you, I will strip
of my clothes and my armor
I would tear the flesh right off the bone
for you, I am naked
for you, I am open

43. reflection

if the moon and the stars are a reflection of the past
would they know how many lifetimes have I been
loving you before our souls reconciled in this one?
because I couldn't possibly have just learned to love you
this much,
all in this single lifetime

44. voice

his voice in my ear
it did intresting things to me
it curveed my back and parted my lips
I felt lazy and feline,
and he wasn't even in the room

45. smile

when he smiles
it is like having a torch
shine right at me
lighting up all the dark corners
and I cannot imagine why everyone
is not in love with him

46. streets and stars

and I could sit with you for hours
tracing the veins along your hand and
counting each birthmark along your back
like streets and stars
in a city made of you
all leading me back to my home;
your heart

47. insane

yeah
maybe I loved
a little insane
but atleast I
had the courage
to lose myself in
something I
truly wanted

48. comfort book

deciding to love you continually
is like reading the same book again
but each time
finding a line that hits deep
and makes me think about something I didn't realize before
and I decide to read it again and again
knowing I'll never get enough of it
knowing I'll aways find something new
about you to love;
your soul is like a comfort book

49. our spot

I still go to our spot
where we used to lay under the stars
away from all our problems
just me & you
though our stars are far apart
somewhere in this world they are shining bright
until our stars collide again
maybe we could shine even brighter as one
I'll wait
as long as it takes

50. cosmos

I shall die before him
I beg of you
whoever is in control-
god, cosmos, nature, ocean
give my body to the sun
so that everytime it finds it's way to his flesh
he is never without the warmth of my love

51. honest

I held his hand in the same way I would hold my keys
with the sole purpose of coming home
except there was no lock on his doors
he let me walk just right in
reserved a seat to the show in the museum
full of everyone he had been
I could've sat front row
as the symphony played;
the annual tragic ballad of the plans he made fade
but I moved onwards
skipping those parts of him like
rocks on water and I thought of how we label ourselves
he's just somebody's son
somebody's friend
somebody's enemy
somebody's could have been something more
somebody's crush
somebody's heartbreak
somebody's double take at a store,
somebody's new beginning
comes with the pressure to have pieces of him away
but our hands interlaced together
makes him a little honest today

52. eyes speak

do you know why our fingers are created distanced apart?
so that the fingers of our loved ones can fill them
no one is sent by accident to anyone
it's all written
if you ever ask me
how many times you've crossed my mind
I would say once
because you came and never left
people are not as beautiful as they look
or as they talk
they are only beautiful as they love
as they care
as they share
the best portion of your life will be the small moments
you spent smiling with someone who matters to you
thinking about you is my hobby
missing you is my concern
caring for you is my job
loving you is my duty
and being there for you is forever a pleasure
we try to hide our feelings
but we forget that our eyes speak

53. incapable

I'm incapable *of tolerating my own heart* without you.

54. hope

he demonstrates how thoughtful it can be
everything is done with purpose
love used to be shopping display windows
while I was drowning beneath the surface
too tired to walk
so he carries me over his shoulder
our memories start to be placed in a
"didn't know I'd laugh this hard" folder
it's fun and exciting
playful like never before
I used to be sobbing but now
we're both cackling on the floor
and if we were words on paper
how melodic would they be?
little miss hopeless romantic might be the very best part of me
a slight hesitation
because nothing ever goes as planned
but suddenly we're walking
and he's reaching to hold my hand
thought I wouldn't feel it
that I gave up long time ago
but he makes me feel like someone
that's very important to know

it's fully deserved and nothing like the past
and I didn't know I'd become
this version of myself so fast
but suddenly here she is
and she radiates like the sun
suddenly it was hard to differentiate
where despair stopped
and hope begun

55. intertwined

I have so much love to give,
that it would overflow if kept in a small container titled "heart."
I tend to make everything about love
because
it is the only thing in the world that truly belongs to me
it fulls void of emptiness in my heart to the brim
I try to look for a place to share it everywhere (and I find it in you),
your heart is where my love would linger, is safe and sound
I can see my love shine through in your presence
your capacity for love knows no bounds for me to pour a little
or more
of my love into it
so let me share my love with you
for love is meant to be cherished by two intertwined souls

56. find me

if one day we are apart
know that I will always remain with you
perhaps I will be the gentle breeze caressing your hair as it
drifts through the window,
the giant tree embracing you with its shade from the blazing
summer sun,
the lily flower blooming beautifully in your mini garden
or the daily newspaper you read with your morning tea every
day
in every little thing
you will find me
for I have left a piece of my heart with you

57. still

and when the years have passed
and we have watched a thousand sunsets
and we are bent
our bodies crooked with age
as me again
in the twilight
in the shadow of the life we have shared
ask me if I love you
and my heart will answer
before my lips can part
my love, my life
my heart never left your hands
always, evermore, even after
still

58. a sin

"you cannot love him", they whisper
"for it's a sin"
I only smile at their words knowing that
they have not knelt at his altar
nor tasted the divinity staining his lips
they have not heard his laugh
murmured between every kiss
"so be it then." I say.
"I will walk into hell gladly
knowing I've held heaven in my hands."

59. open book

he's like an open book
everyone thinks they know him
but some pages are torn
the parts he doesn't let anyone see
the parts that I have seen
the parts I don't want anyone most about him forever
I want to memorize every page of his book
every word
I want to hold him the way you hold a book
with a certain delicacy
the way one knows never to step over a book
though he has let people step over him
but as long as I live
I won't let that happen any more
because I'll hold him the way every book deserves to be held
his spine is broken
one too many times
cracks, tears
but I'll trace my fingers over his spine
and try to heal him
I'll hold the pages that are torn
and put them back into his book
because they make him him

whether or not he's proud of them

because I am proud of each page

torn or not torn

60. ocean love

loving you is like the ocean
it's deep and very long
it's wide and sometimes quiet
but underneath it's very strong
loving you is the salty air
that breezes down the coast
it's the beauty in the details
and the sand between our toes
loving you is jumping in
without knowing first the chill
it's give and take and build and brake
it's fighting through all the feels
loving you is surfing waves
calm, but throws you hard
it's the breath you take when you've been under
it's the bright damp towels in your car
loving you is the ocean
it goes for miles in all directions
you could sink for hours and still never know
the weight of my affections
and just how deep my feelings grow
so finally when you reach the floor
the ocean learns our memories

all we've made and all the more

the ocean knows just what you mean

the ocean knows all the you and me

the ocean knows we're lovely

61. peace

his smile was hiding secrets
I dared to know more about
tired looking eyes
eyes that crave affection, but the love is lost
they were not matching his soft
heart-warming smile whilst not meeting mine
a smile played on his heart shaped lips
each time we locked our eyes
at that precise moment
time stopped in a collision of senses
the outside world got blurry
as if we were the only ones whose existence is known
among 7.9 billion people his smile
will always be my favourite
a smile that made me forget all my stress and worries
could melt every time
the wrinkles on his face whenever he smiled
emphasized his cheeks so pronounced
impossible not to be all smiles
I found peace in it

62. moon

he looks like the moon
not like the stars amongst the same
not like the sun, to flashy to face
just like the moon
just like a garden filled with roses and luck
every feature on his face represents the phase a moon has
his smile is a waning crescent
and on occasion it's a waxing crescent
I do love myself and I know that I'm not always half
but on days when I feel like a third quater
he's there to be my first
our birth moons don't complete each other
but for me it doesn't matter
cause if he can be the full moon
then I'll be willing to be the new
even if he will be the only one to shine
even if his roses dies and his luck runs out
I will be there and the last standing rose
holding the last glass of luck
then give it all to the moon

63. the world is ours

being with you
is like dancing in the rain
no thoughts in my head
except the way
the water drips against your skin
laughing so loud
like the world is ours
heart shaped clouds
high in the sky
just me and you
stealing glances and kisses
they make me tipsy
my heart is pounding with joy
because darling,
love with you
is like love with no other

64. love leaves leftovers

it's been three years and I still have the french keyboard
enabled on my phone
occasionally, when I comment on the poems on the internet
it autocorrects *love* to *liberte*
it's been three years and I still sleep facing the window
because it's good to feel the sun when you wake
everytime I see a squirrel
I think of how you, completely amazed by their existence
tried to feed them peanuts off your balcony railing
and how they came to you and gently nuzzled your hands
I've never shit-talked squirrels since
love leaves leftovers, I've learned
it's never a clean escape
oh but what a way to say goodbye:
here, *I've loved you,*
save some for later

65. hour glass

if everything you touch
turns to dust
I will be the sand
trapped in the hour glass
on your desk
admiring you
with each passing second
with each passing grain of sand

66. birthday pizza

beneath a sky where twilight fades to night
we sat with ice cream on the terrace, cool and sweet
our laughter mingling with the stars' soft light
a summer's dream where hearts and memories meet
we watched the sunset paint the world in gold
captured moments
snapshots of our bliss with every kiss
our love story unfolds
in endless kisses, time ceased to exist
on birthdays, pizza shared with tender smiles
sneaking out to greet the dawn's first rays
cooking meals, our love in every spice
these cherished times
our hearts in sweet embrace
in every glance, in every whispered word
our love's a symphony that's deeply heard

67. I miss you

so I might
count every star
to where you are
and write you
metaphors in millions
with all the skies
but really,
you just need to know;
I miss you
I've still never seen stars
like the ones in your eyes

68. we are the stars

I was once told that humans

are made of stardust

which is to say,

that there is a chance

that the lovers

those who are our soulmates

are just smaller pieces of the same star

when

the Big

met

The Bang

and science happened before eyes that did not exist yet

collided and made love to each other

was your star next to mine?

tell me, my love;

did someone ever wish upon the star we are made from?

69. firefly

there are things I can't control
and memories I can never erase
and in the times I don't feel whole,
I will always search for your face
you are every star burning in the sky
you are every golden leaf in the tallest tree
you are a pattern, a snowflake, and every firefly
and I will still love you even when we're eighty-three
I will stand by you in every new day
even when people seem so unkind
because you are beautiful despite what they say
and you are everything I've wanted to find
for all the places in which we will go
for one day you might be my one
I think we both already know
I am yours in every life

70. big bang

I fell in love with you way before we met
was it when we took our first steps?
or was it when the universe got created?
I think it was the big bang,
that scattered the stars
which faded under the light you radiated
I think it was the sun which burned so hard because
it couldn't shine as bright as you are
I think it was the moon that got scarred from your perfection
I think it was the black hole which couldn't consume the
celestial lights
you hold in the crooks of your body
I think it was the universe which got numb from your
oh so melodious voice
I think it was then, I fell for you

71. family recipe

my family still uses the recipes
our ancestors left behind
it is believed in the olden days
you could identify a family
simply by looking at a recipe
the need to be known is
an ancient desire
I didn't start cooking before I met you
my breakfast were often store bought and refrigerated
now softening the onion in the butter is
almost as easy as knowing you
I want to be remembered by you

72. gone

I AM SO IN LOVE WITH YOU I WANT TO LIE DOWN IN THE MIDDLE OF A MAJOR PUBLIC INTERSECTION AND CRY
is not how you are supposed to start love poems
but I'm too far gone
to work up to it gently

73. take me by the throat

if he wanted to dance
I would let him wreck the furniture
if he wanted to cook
I would let him burn down the house
and if he wanted to scream
I would let him deafen me
I've never loved anyone enough to let them destroy me
but God,
he could take me by the throat
and my eyes would sparkle at the mere inches between us

74. in my dreams

I choose to love you in silence
for in silence I find no rejection
I choose to love you in loneliness
for in loneliness no one owns you but me
I choose to adore you from a distance
for distance will shield me from pain
I choose to kiss you in the wind
for the wind is gentler than my lips
I choose to hold you in my dreams
for in my dreams, you have no end

75. future

I will save a spot for you in my future
when I map out a plan for the life I hope to one day live
I'll carve a little spot out for you in every version of it
just in case you ever decide you want to be part of it again
there will always be room for you here

76. burned

then you kissed me-
It felt hot wax on my forehead
I wanted it to leave a mark:
that's how I knew I loved you.
because I wanted to be burned, stamped,
to have something in the end-

77. secret

the longer I was around him,
the more I could see the colors of his mind and the recesses of
his heart
there was a beast in there
but there was also a boy who was afraid of being a beast
and who wondered if other people had beasts in their hearts
too
there was strength,
and there was also just the determination to look strong
he guarded himself like a secret

78. tags

so, take my tags, and I'll take yours,
and if I die in this shitty fucking war
don't tell them we switched;
let me be buried under your name-
and some fifty years from now,
you can be buried under mine

79. violent

"You don't truly love someone until they've hurt you and you
still think of them as the greatest person in the world. Love is
the most violent act"
when wounds are fresh and tears still fall,
when echoes of their words still call
you find within your heart,
a place where love for them remains with grace
in moments when the pain is fierce,
when memories cut deep and pierce
you see their flaws, their human side
yet cherish them with boundless pride
for love is not a gentle breeze,
it's storms and tempests, wild seas
a force that breaks then heals anew
a dance of pain and beauty too
so when you think of them and smile
despite the hurt, it's all worthwhile
for love, in it's most violent form
transforms the heart, a raging storm
and in that chaos, you will find
a love that's pure
a love that's blind
for only through the trials we face

do we embrace love's fierce embrace

80. waiting

am I in love ?-
yes, since I'm waiting
the other never waits
sometimes I want to play the part of the one who doesn't wait;
I try to busy myself elsewhere, to arrive late;
but I always lose at this game:
whatever I do, I find myself there, with nothing to do,
punctual, even ahead of time
the lover's fatal identity is precisely;
I am the one who waits

81. grief

how powerfully I carry him within me
my grief is tremendous
but my love,
my love is bigger

82. bones

I wanted his bones, his blood, his tissues, the sinews that
bound him together
I would have held him to me though time had stripped away
the tones amd textures of his skin
I could have held him for a thousand years until the skeleton
itself rubbed away to dust
what are you that makes me feel thus?
who are you for whom time has no meaning?
in the heat of his hands I thought,
this is the campfire that mocks the sun
this place will warm me, feed me and care for me
I will hold on to this pulse against other rhytms
the world will come and go in the tide of a day
but here is his hand with my future in it's palm

83. power

I am woven into his veins.
Our bond was forged in seawater and ash.
Tell me, when you kissed his pretty mouth,
did you taste my power too?

84. my person

he puts his hands on either side of my face and the room falls
away
I have never gotten so lost in a kiss before
and then, the space between us explodes
my heart keeps missing beats and my hands cannot bring him
close enough to me
I taste him and realize I have been starving
I have loved before, but it didn't feel like this
I have kissed before, but it didn't burn me alive
maybe it lasts a minute, and maybe it's an hour
all I know is that kiss,
and how soft his skin is when it brushes against mine
and that even if I did not know it until now,
I have been waiting for this person forever

85. pure

pure, and i mean that:
his hair touching my arm as he sleeps
imagine feeling that safe
I can
I do
the terror of all times stops
the night freezes
he shifts quietly but doesn't wake
soft midnight breathing like a blue hammock
paradisiacal
everything evil becomes bearable
and I think,
I've loved you the whole of my life, which isn't possible
my life only started *when I loved you,*
which is

86. sacred

it torments me to see you for just a few hours and then
surrender you
when I see you all that I wanted to say vanishes -
the time is so precious and words are extraneous
but you make me so happy- because I can talk to you
I love your brightness, your preparations for flight,
your legs like a vise, the warmth between your legs
yes, I want to demask you
I am too gallant with you
I want to look at you long and ardently
pick up your clothes, fondle you, examine you
do you know I have scarcely looked at you?
there is still too much sacredness clinging to you

87. shiver

you say my name and I want to knit
my bones into your bones, smooth away
the boundaries of our heartbeats
what I'm trying to say is that if the temperature
inside those wild pockets of interstellar
dust hits right near absolute zero
carbon monoxide and dilhydrogen
molecules condense together in the dark
nebula to form stars
if you're ready,
I want to make you shiver like that

88. beautiful

I've never believed that beauty could exist in self destruction.
then I saw you
and your eyes told stories with dangerous beginnings and lost
endings
where every page was breathing with color
yes, you were beautiful to me

89. twinkling

I think the moon is the reflection of your eyes;
how it gleams so tenderly in the dark and these reminded me
of your twinkling eyes,
it made me feel lovely that even amidst the quietness I didn't
feel lonely
it's beam is spilling over my skin and it makes me feel seen
I think I've fallen for you again for the umpteenth time
well, it's not like I stopped loving you seconds ago, no
it's just that, any time I wake up to a beautiful thing I fall for you
more;
because you remind me of each and all of it
you remind me of every little beautiful thing that keeps me
going
every and all that gave me hope to keep on living
my dear darling, tonight, too, the moon is beaming, and now
I can't help but think about your lovely eyes that never stop
twinkling

90. flesh

I am yours;
with every inch of flesh
and bone in my
body; and every ounce of love
instilled
in me, I belong to you
with every subtle thought
that slips my
mind; and every void space in my empty soul,
I belong to you

91. kindness

when I think of you, my breath becomes yours
and my pain no longer hurts
you are the kindness my life has never had
you are the love my parents could never show me
you are the next day covered in golden flesh that will keep the
night
in company when all the stars fall asleep

92. sensations

my skin is yours, sweet soul
when the rain falls on you
I feel it swimming through me
when the sun sneaks out of the clouds to kiss you and hide
again
I feel your lips upon mine
when a new universe collides with you
the crumbling will devour us both
I cannot see a day where I'd ever wish to feel the sensations
of the earth without you

93. dance

when you danced with me that night
something strange happened
I felt as if a blazing star
left it's place in the sky
and sought refuge in my chest
I felt as if an entire forest
was growing under my clothes
I felt as if a three-year-old child
was writing her schoolwork
on the fabric of my shirt
it is not my habit to dance
but that night
I was not merely dancing
I was the dance

94. yours and mine

life is yours, death is mine
peace is yours, stress is mine
happiness is yours, sorrow is mine
everything is yours
but you are mine

95. things that fall

petals

teardrops

snowflakes

rain

stars

tides

eyelids

time

shadows

leaves

the sun

and I,

for you

96. penetrate

he gets me tipsy on words

letters dress my skin

until my blood is flustered

heart beat at race

and butterflies roam around every ribcage

blushing

fingertips dance

across my body until

I am

drunk on his aroma

warmth blankets me with goosebumps

hard.

it's how he penetrates me

slow.

it's how he fills me

97. drown

I've gotten so good
about not flinching at the sound of your name
that people don't know I'd still throw myself
mouth-open into the ocean
for the chance to drown somewhere you might see it

98. memory

I can't look into your eyes
but they're all I think about
I memorized your face as if it's my mirror
or a prayer that needs to be said every night
I will forget my name
before I forget you

99. candlelight dinner

I want to love you at your family's candlelit dinner table
as the snow falls slowly outside
at one point, your relatives will ask about our story
I'll have to refrain from telling them that you've painted stars
across my soul- that is a secret I'll confess to you
under the covers, and to the moon later in the night
and when the noise becomes too loud
I'll touch your pinky, bump into your knee
delicately remind you that I'm here
that I can hear you, always

100. i love you

I choose you, when the rain is heavy or the sun is light

I choose you; if it is just not my day and I am sad

I choose you, or I am happy and the stars shine bright, I choose you

I choose you in the good and the bad, in the seasons of joy or the seasons of sorrow

I choose you

I choose to stand with you, and to grow together

I will not be found in the sun without you by my side because

I CHOOSE YOU

I am here

and I choose you to be with me through it all

Author's Note

When I started writing this book, I was filled with a different feeling than I had while I'm reaching the end pages. Though the circumstances have changed, the essence of those memories remains captured within these pages and my heart. We often forget the value of our loved ones. Today you have your mom telling you to keep your shoes in place and the next time you're sitting alone in a room of mess and grief of the person long gone. We often assume tomorrow will bring another chance to say "I love you" or to hold them close. But life is fragile, and one day, without warning, the people who fill our hearts may no longer be there. So let your love be known. Speak the words you often hold back, embrace them with warmth, and create memories that will linger long after they're gone. It's the little things that matter- the shared smiles, the quiet moments, the laughter that echoes in your heart. Please, I urge you to value them before they are long gone and just a memory.

As I close the chapters of this book, my heart overflows with gratitude for each of you. Thank you for allowing my words to intertwine with your feelings.